I0256266

It Will Be Ok

By Missy Yeska

Amazing illustrations and book design also by the author (sketched hurriedly in the morning before her children woke up - hence all the imperfections...
kind of like motherhood!)

Copyright © 2019 by Melissa Scalise

All rights reserved. No part of this publication may be reproduced, distributed, or transmitted in any form or by any means, including photocopying, recording, or other electronic or mechanical methods, without the prior written permission of the publisher, except in the case of brief quotations embodied in critical reviews and certain other noncommercial uses permitted by copyright law.

ISBN: 978-1-7340134-0-5

- To Katie and all new moms

'It will be ok' will hopefully become your mantra or your battle-cry (depending on the day!)

*10% of profit will benefit organizations supporting women with postpartum mood disorders

-Hi, Mom!

Mom, I can't wait to meet you! I have been spending a lot of time listening to and studying your voice. Your walk rocks me to sleep. I know you will be an amazing mommy.

There are just a few things I want to make sure you understand before I come. First of all, I will love you no matter what. I don't expect you to be perfect. If you can't make homemade organic baby food, that's ok. If you let me have 30 more minutes of screen time than is recommended, that's ok, too. I haven't met them yet, but I assume your parents weren't perfect, and you turned out pretty well.

As long as you love me and create a safe space for me, it will be ok.

You are the perfect parent for me!

When you meet me, it may be butterflies and rainbows and love at first sight. This is normal. However, it's also normal to not experience butterflies and rainbows at first. Some parents don't feel an immediate bond with their newborn. If this happens to us, don't worry. Our bond will develop over time. We're in this together.

It will be ok.

This is just between you and me, but I will be fine whether you bottle or breastfeed me. Really, I will be. This is your decision and a very personal one. It is no one's business what you choose or for how long.

It will be ok.

There will be other people taking care of me (possibly my other parent, your friends, grandparents, etc.) They will not do things the way you do them. As long as they're not hurting me, let them do it their way. To be honest, I like variety and learning to trust other people.

Mom, you need to be able to tell other people what YOU need. Sometimes that can be hard to do, but it's not only important for your sanity, it's also important for me. I need to learn how to tell others what I need, too, and I do that first by watching you.

It will be ok.

Ok, Mom, this is serious. If you have postpartum depression, please ask for help. This occurs in 10% of women and stems from sleep deprivation and hormonal changes that are out of your control. If you are feeling sad a lot or feel yourself losing interest in things, please talk about it with your doctor. Postpartum anxiety isn't discussed as much as postpartum depression, but it is also serious. Please also discuss it with your doctor if you experience this.

As long as you recognize these situations and get help if you need it, it will be ok.

Mom, I am wreaking some havoc on your body. Your clothes won't fit the same. You may never be able to jump on a trampoline again! I am super-sorry about that. Of course, I am totally worth it, though.

It will be ok.

1. Feed the baby
2. Change the baby
3. Survive

Mom, people will tell you to sleep when you can. This is good advice but completely impossible. I basically will take up all your time--all of it--especially in the beginning. Just do your best. At the beginning, your only goal for the day should be to make sure I am fed and my diapers are changed. If you get a shower or do some laundry, you are way ahead of the game, and that is a bonus.

It will be ok.

Don't listen to advice (other than what you read in this book, of course!) No one else is me, and no one else is you. What works for one baby doesn't necessarily work for another. I will sleep through the night when I am destined to sleep through the night, and no amount of standing on your head and patting your belly while singing a lullaby will help me.

You can try some ideas you read about in books and that your doctor recommends if you want, but if they don't work, just understand that I may not be a baby that sleeps well. It's possible I won't sleep through the night the whole first year. It's also possible that I'll start at 12 weeks.

The people who say their baby sleeps through the night at six weeks either are very lucky they had a baby that tends to sleep well--or--they are lying! Just be patient and know that this will pass.

It will be ok.

self-doubt
Second Guess
Guilt

Mom, now this is really serious. It doesn't matter whether you stay at home or whether you go back to work part- or full-time, you will have guilt. You will feel guilty for not being with me if you go back to work. You will feel guilty if you stay at home. You will feel guilty if you don't make stuffed elves do crazy things every single day during the holidays. You will feel guilty if you do things for yourself. You will feel guilty the first time I get hurt, etc., etc., etc. This is normal. All mothers feel it to some degree. There will be positives and negatives associated with every decision you make.

Please decide what is important to our family and do that.

Don't look back. Don't second-guess. Don't compare.

It will be ok.

Judgment-free zone

Mom, please don't judge other mommies. It will be easy to do. There will be decisions that you make and feel are better than different decisions that other moms make, but remember what works for us doesn't work for everyone. Moms are all just doing their best. Just be and let others be. Don't give advice unless someone asks. Listen and be open-minded. There will be a time when you are judged, and it will feel yucky. Don't let other moms who are doing their best feel yucky.

It will be ok.

Mom, I can't wait to get to know each other and learn from each other. I am so lucky to have you! Just remember, it will truly all be ok as long as you create a safe space for me and love me. You are the perfect mom for me.

www.ingramcontent.com/pod-product-compliance
Lightning Source LLC
Chambersburg PA
CBHW040759150426
42811CB00055B/1072